The Amdahl Graphics

Graphics

... 1974
... 1975
... 1976

Raymond St Arnaud

Published by
Raymond St. Arnaud
Victoria, British Columbia, Canada
www.raymondstarnaud.com
starnaud@shaw.ca

Photographs, Manipulation, Design, Layout and Pre-Press by
Raymond St. Arnaud

Second Edition

ISBN: 978-14499692-4-0

To my wife Liz

I wouldn't be here, if it were not for you.

Other books by Raymond St. Arnaud

27 after 25
A book of photographs documenting 27 instructors and celebrating their
25 years of service. 60 pages, 54 photographs, 978-1-4499689-2-2, 2005

As Seen on TV
A book of Digital prints, based on manipulated photographs, that are cultural
representations of TV images.
40 pages, 15 full images, 15 detail images, ISBN: 978-1-4499689-6-0, 2007

Outside the Box
A book of Digital prints, based on manipulated photographs, that echo traditional
printmaking techniques. 54 pages, 42 images, ISBN 978-1-4499690-3-5, 2007

Reflections: The Pre-Millennium Landscapes
A book of photographs that are an experimental semi-abstract series, grounded in
the
cultural and economic fabric of North American society in the 20th century.
134 pages, 120 photographs, ISBN 978-1-4499690-9-7, 2007

The Camosun Photos
A book of photographs produced while employed by Camosun College, Victoria,
BC, Canada. 140 pages, 274 photographs, ISBN 978-0-9738256-8-8, 2007

The Dysfunctional Photographer
A book of photographs from one of two blogs, each featuring a new photograph
every day for 100 days. The photographs are based on normal day-to-day life
experiences. 114 pages, 100 photographs, ISBN: 978-1-4499691-6-5, 2008

The Forced March
A book of photographs from one of two blogs, each featuring a new photograph
every day for 100 days. The photographs are based on normal day-to-day life
experiences. 114 pages, 100 photographs, ISBN 978-1-4499691-5-8, 2008

Secrets . . . from the Museums of Paris
One of three books of photographs from *the french collection*. This book dwells on aspects of the museums normally ignored by most visitors, and features images with altered states of colour, contrast and detail.
104 pages, 86 photographs, ISBN 978-1-4499596-4-7, 2008

Sortie . . . The Running Man
One of three books of photographs from *the french collection*. This book documents "Sortie" signs and their immediate environment in Paris museums, and features images with altered states of colour, contrast and detail. 8 pages, 51 photographs, ISBN 978-1-4499610-7-7, 2008

Random Walks . . . Paris
One of three books of photographs from *the french collection*. This book encompasses day-to-day experiences while wandering around Paris and features common themes that evolved during the experience.
144 pages, 123 photographs, ISBN978-1-4499608-4-1, 2008

Visit...to a Surrey Townhouse
An exercise in discovery and spontaneous exploration in a small townhouse located in Surrey, BC, Canada. The images feature further exploration of the world of exaggerated colour and contrast.
50 pages, 37 photographs, ISBN 978-1-4499691-0-3, 2008

Frank Gurney . . . engraver
A 40th anniversary project based on photographs of Frank Gurney in 1969. News of Frank as the engraver for replicas of the Grey Cup, the symbol of supremacy in the Canadian Football League, led to the resurrection of the negatives. New photographs from 2009 have been added to the collection. 58 pages, 44 photographs, ISBN: 978-1-4499692-7-1, 2009

About the Artist

Raymond St. Arnaud has been active as a photographer, painter and printmaker since 1968. He has exhibited extensively in solo, shared and group shows in thirty-one states in the United States and in British Columbia, Alberta and Ontario in Canada.

Work in permanent collections:

Ottawa, Ontario
> Library & Archives Canada/Bibliothèque & Archives Canada
> Canadian Museum of Contemporary Photography

Calgary, Alberta
> Esso Resources
> Energy Resources Conservation Board

Edmonton, Alberta
> YMCA

San Diego, California
> San Diego Art Institute

Grand Junction, Colorado
> Johnson Gallery, Mesa State College

He has also exhibited in web galleries centered on computer imaging conferences in Australia, China, Thailand, Spain, Switzerland, the United Kingdom and the United States.

Table of Contents

Preface x

The Transparents

    The Transparents, No. 1 3

    The Transparents, No. 2 4

    The Transparents, No. 3 5

The Contours

    The Contours, No. 1 7

    The Contours, No. 2 8

    The Contours, No. 3 9

    The Contours, No. 4 10

    The Contours, No. 5 11

The Flights

    The Flights, No. 1 13

    The Flights, No. 2 14

    The Flights, No. 3 15

    The Flights, No. 4 16

The Verticals

    The Verticals, No. 1 18

    The Verticals, No. 2 19

    The Verticals, No. 3 20

    The Verticals, No. 4 21

    The Verticals, No. 5 22

    The Verticals, No. 6 23

    The Verticals, No. 7 24

The Chaotics

The Chaotics, No. 1 26
The Chaotics, No. 2 27
The Chaotics, No. 3 28
The Chaotics, No. 4 29
The Chaotics, No. 5 30

The Figuratives

04-08-75, Digit 1904 32
04-08-75, Digit 1908 33
11-27-75, Digit 5751 34
11-27-75, Digit 8240 35
12-17-75, Digit 8790 36
12-17-75, Digit 8791 37
12-17-75, Digit 8801 38
01-07-76, Digit 9345 39
01-07-76, Digit 9346 40
01-07-76, Digit 9351 41
01-09-76, Digit 9448 42
01-09-76, Digit 9531 43
01-14-76, Digit 9623 44
02-25-76, Digit 1398 45
03-31-76, Digit 3420 46
03-31-76, Digit 3434 47
04-15-76, Digit 4308 48
04-15-76, Digit 4309 49
04-15-76, Digit 4310 50
04-17-76, Digit 4311 51
04-17-76, Digit 4314 52
05-03-76, Digit 5371 53
05-03-76, Digit 5388 54
05-04-76, Digit 5389 55
05-04-76, Digit 5390 56

05-04-76, Digit 5392 57
05-04-76, Digit 5395 58
05-06-76, Digit 5524 59
05-06-76, Digit 5530 60
05-06-76, Digit 5533 61
05-06-76, Digit 5534 62
05-06-76, Digit 5538 63
05-06-76, Digit 5567 64
05-10-76, Digit 5689 65

Preface

The Accidental Progression

In 1974 I was a student at the University of Alberta, Edmonton, taking courses in Fine Arts and Psychology. On one occasion I fulfilled a Fine Arts assignment with what I thought was an elegant and simple solution that required graphically comparing two variables. The instructor challenged me to come up with a solution that dealt with more variables.

Challenges usually drive me to the nearest coffee shop to ponder the possibilities. I visualized a solution, but concluded that calculating multiple variables was beyond my grasp. I reported to my department that it could be done with the assistance of a computer to do the processing.

The Fine Arts department had a computer budget, but had little need of it. The only computer use at that time was for typesetting.

Given my lack of programming skills, I was fortunate to find Ken Bailey, who was taking Industrial Design courses. Ken had been an engineering student and had learned a bit of Fortran. I described what I wanted to create: a cube with mathematical functions on four sides and the ability to merge these functions across the interior space of the cube. Ken found a public domain program and modified it for my needs. He showed me how to control the variables. I was off on my first computer graphics adventure.

I pursued this path through 1974 and into 1975, using the university's Amdahl mainframe computer. My original intent was soon lost. The creation of computer generated graphics went beyond the normal course requirements and became an end of its own. I was grateful for the financing that allowed me to pursue this interest. I've always hoped the Fine Arts department was happy to see someone using their computer budget.

Reimbursement Leads to the Figuratives

In late 1975 I was to be reimbursed for lost photographs from an art show organized by the Fine Arts department in another city. I took payment in computer dollars instead. No longer registered as a student, the computer dollars allowed me access to the Amdahl and its facilities.

I had discovered the digitizer earlier. It was a large scale version of what we now call a Wacom Tablet. It had been built by the University of Alberta's computing division. This large device, a drafting table with sensors built in, was typically used to digitize maps.

The digitizer process became the basis for graphics in the second half of this book, the Figurative drawings. The original images were selected from my perceived personal environment, which at the time consisted of the content of
magazines and newspapers.

I would create the initial drawing on paper and turn it in to the service desk. A staff person would use the digitizer, trace out the drawing and create a computer file. The file was then output using a pen plotter to draw on paper. I gravitated to using a digitizing variable that would read all the points that passed under the cursor, but only recorded a chosen percentage of the points. The result was a series of straight lines, joined at odd angles that defined the figure.

I thought it interesting to have several random events in the process. First, the random presentation and subsequent choices of original images. Second, the choices made by the operator when he/she recorded my original drawings. Third, the randomness of the plotted points.

I was in a state committed to removing the hand of the artist from the artwork. The computer generated drawings were used as models for hard edge paintings, painted with the use of masking tape and watered down acrylic paint to produce a flat, even surface.

The Amdahl Graphics

... 1974
... 1975
... 1976

Raymond St Arnaud

obvious

guileless

The Transparents

pellucid

crystal clear

limpid

lucid

crystalline

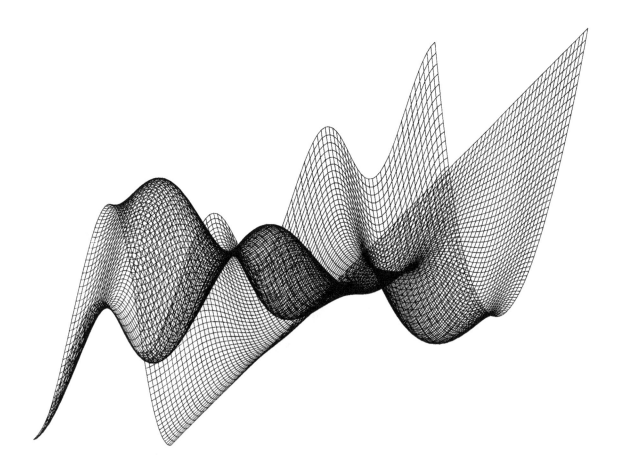

The Transparents, No. 1   *3*

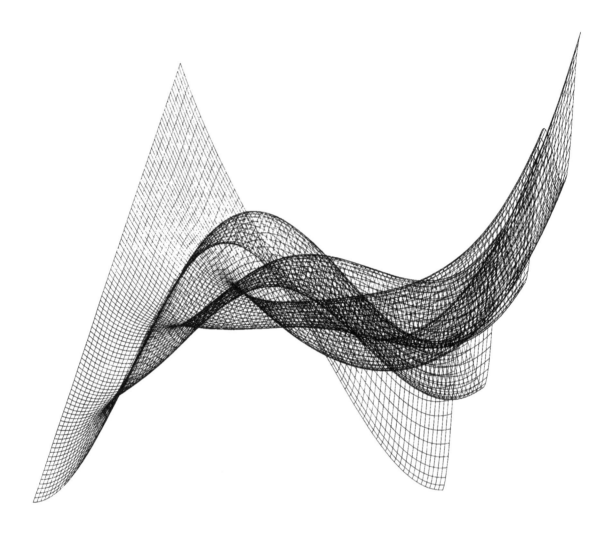

4   The Transparents, No. 2

The Transparents, No. 3   5

shape

form

conformation

configuration

characteristic

The Contours

contour line

feature

outline

delineate

limn

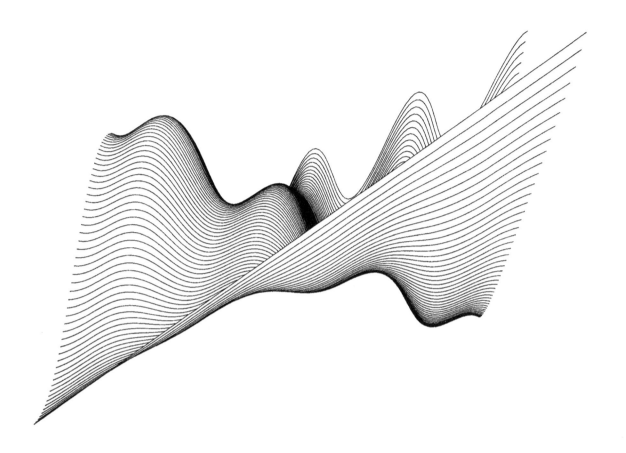

The Contours, No. 1

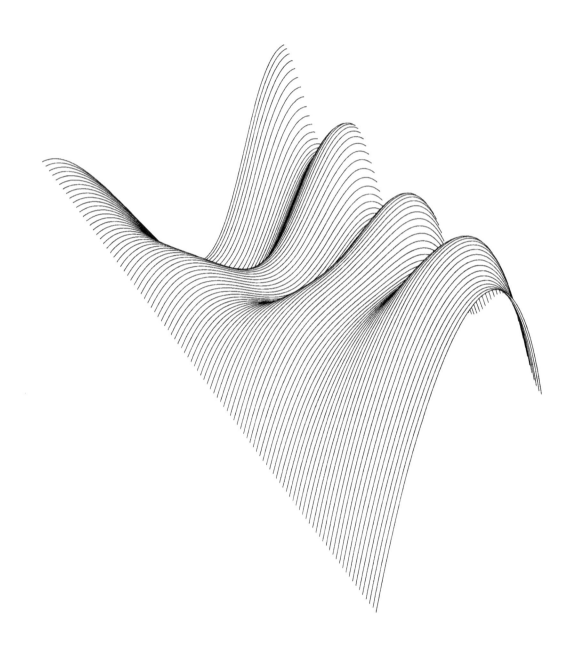

The Contours, No. 2

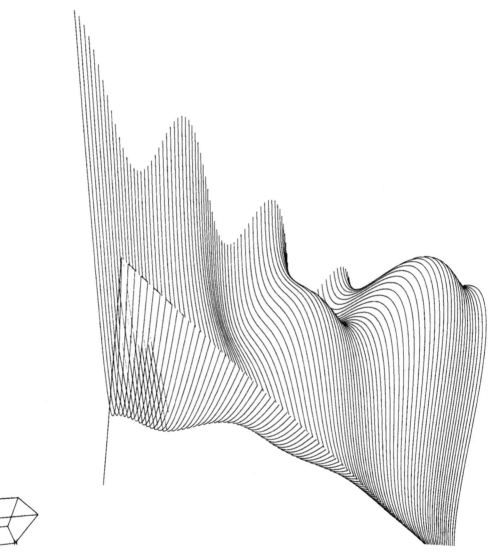

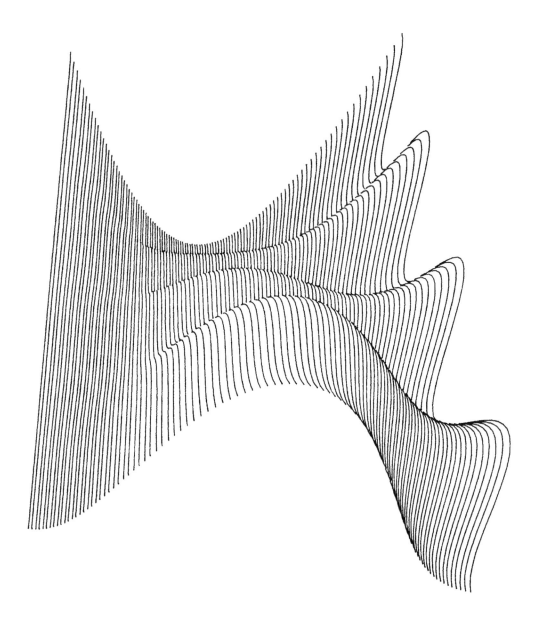

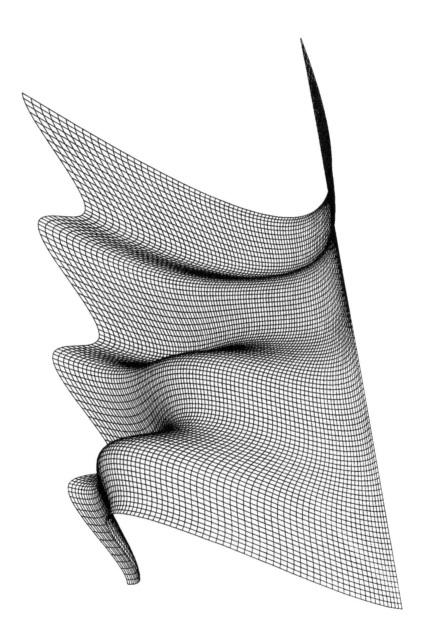

The Contours, No. 5   *11*

steps

trajectory

fledge

stairs

wing

trip

The Flights

pip

escape

shoot

flee

formation

flock

fly

creative

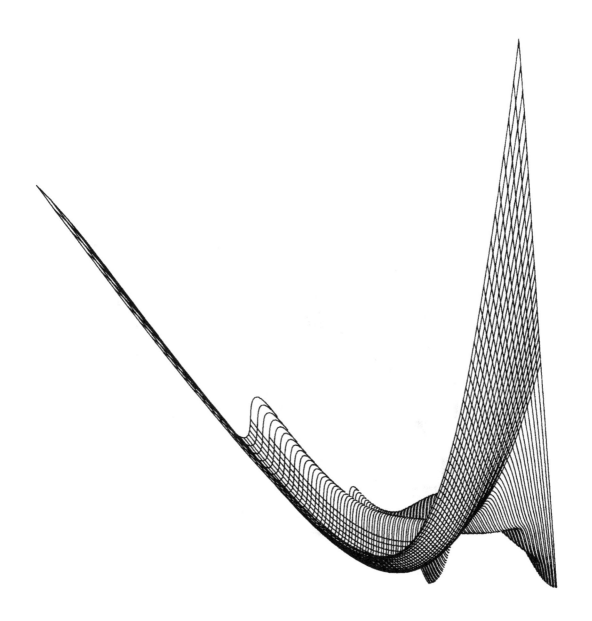

The Flights, No. 1   *13*

14   The Flights, No. 2

The Flights, No. 3

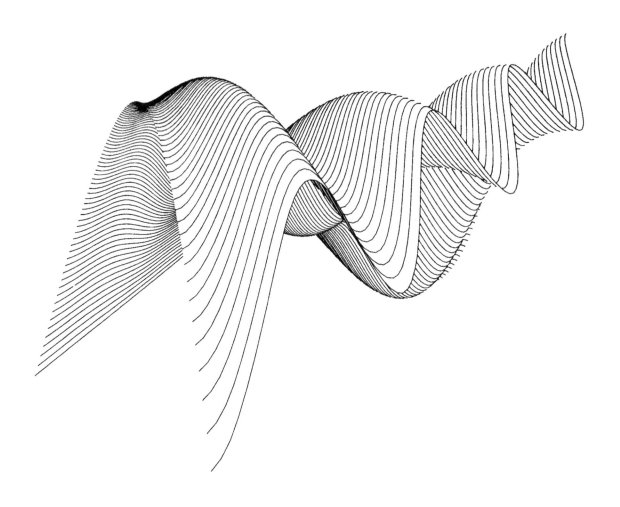

16   The Flights, No. 4

upright

erect

inclined

The Verticals

orientation

perpendicular

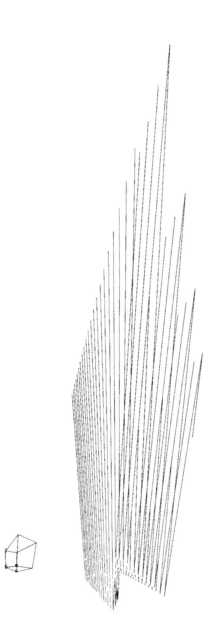

The Verticals, No. 1

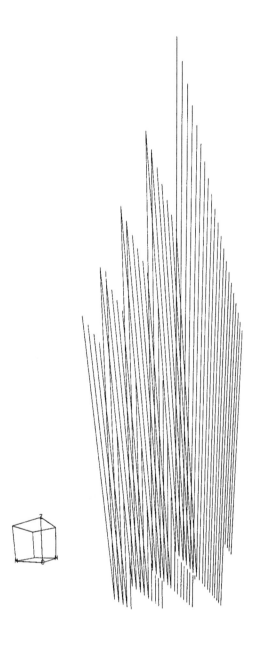

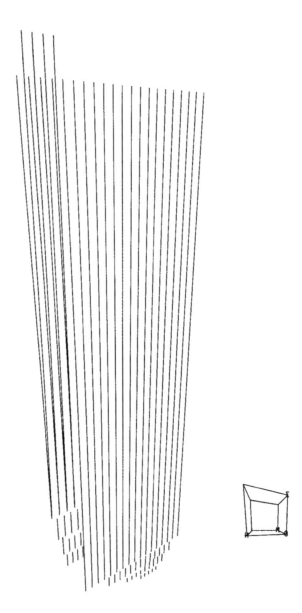

The Verticals, No. 3

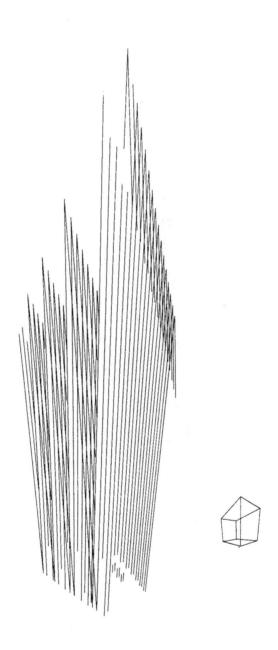

The Verticals, No. 4

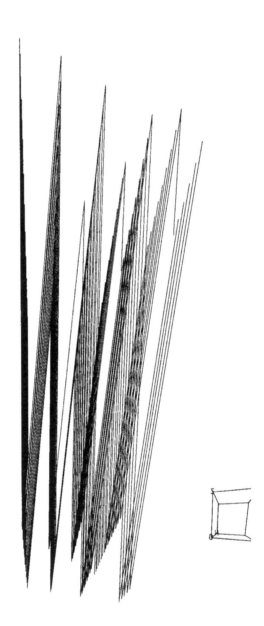

The Verticals, No. 5

The Verticals, No. 6

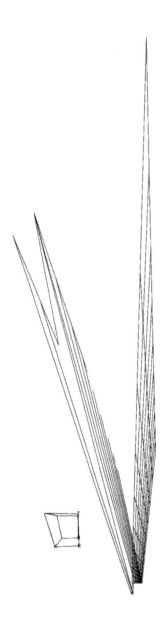

The Verticals, No. 7

dynamical
system

bedlam

physical
phenomenon

The Chaotics

greek deity

pandemonium

topsy-turvy

chaos

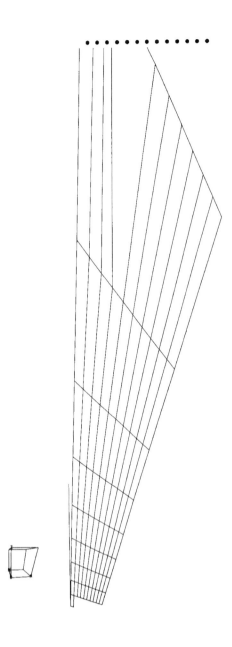

The Chaotics, No. 1

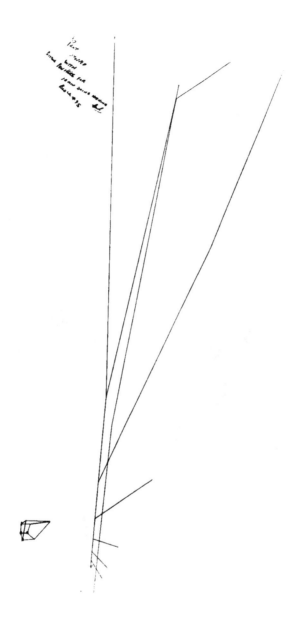

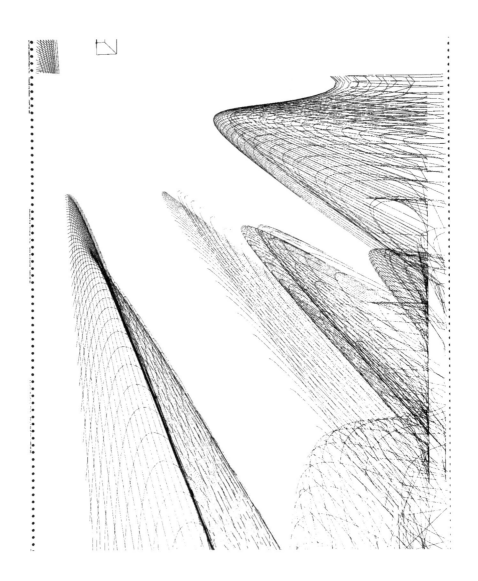

The Chaotics, No. 3

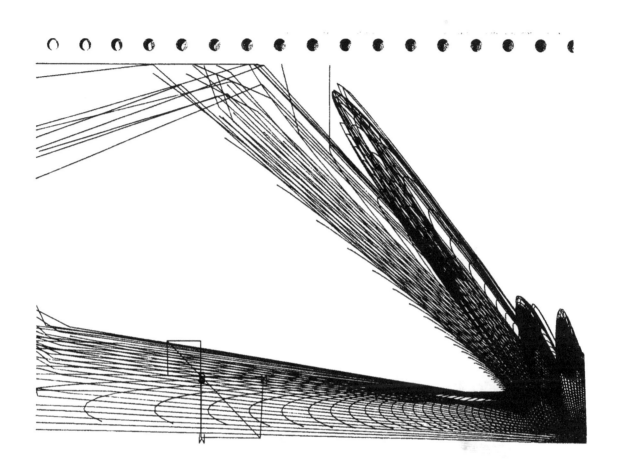

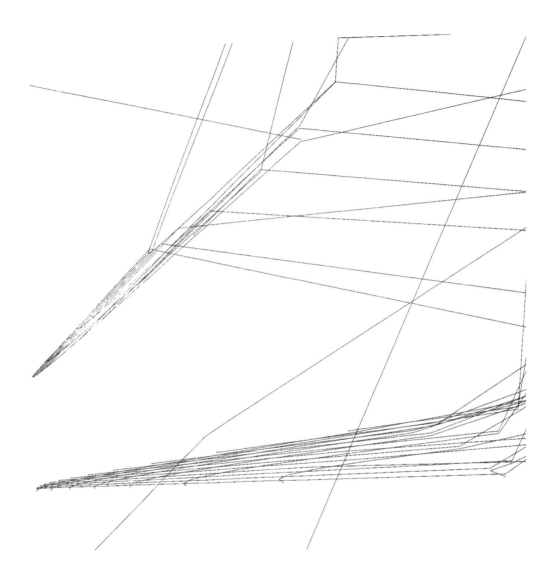

allegorical

denotative

figural

metaphorical

descriptive

illustrative

The Figuratives

fanciful

flowery

representative

emblematic

non-literal

ornate

pictorial

The Figuratives, 04-08-75, Digit 1908   *33*

The Figuratives, 11-27-75, Digit 5751

The Figuratives, 11-27-75, Digit 8240   *35*

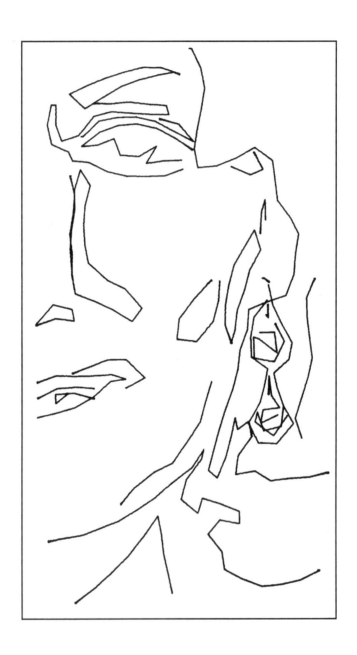

36   The Figuratives, 12-17-75, Digit 8790

The Figuratives, 12-17-75, Digit 8791   *37*

　　　The Figuratives, 01-07-7, Digit 8801

The Figuratives, 01-07-76, Digit 9345

The Figuratives, 01-07-76, Digit 9346

The Figuratives, 01-07-76, Digit 9351 *41*

42   The Figuratives, 01-09-76, Digit 9448

The Figuratives, 01-09-76, Digit 9531 *43*

The Figuratives, 01-14-76, Digit 9623

The Figuratives, 02-25-76, Digit 1398

46   The Figuratives, 03-31-76, Digit 3434

The Figuratives, 03-31-76, Digit 3420

48   The Figuratives, 04-15-76, Digit 4308

The Figuratives, 04-15-76, Digit 4309

The Figuratives, 04-15-76, Digit 4310

The Figuratives, 04-17-76, Digit 4311

52   The Figuratives, 04-17-76, Digit 4314

The Figuratives, 05-03-76, Digit 5371   *53*

The Figuratives, 05-03-76, Digit 5388

The Figuratives, 05-04-76, Digit 5389   *55*

The Figuratives, 05-04-76, Digit 5390

The Figuratives, 05-04-76, Digit 5392

The Figuratives, 05-04-76, Digit 5395

The Figuratives, 05-06-76, Digit 5524   *59*

The Figuratives, 05-06-76, Digit 5530

The Figuratives, 05-06-76, Digit 5533   *61*

The Figuratives, 05-06-76, Digit 5567

The Figuratives, 05-10-76, Digit 5689